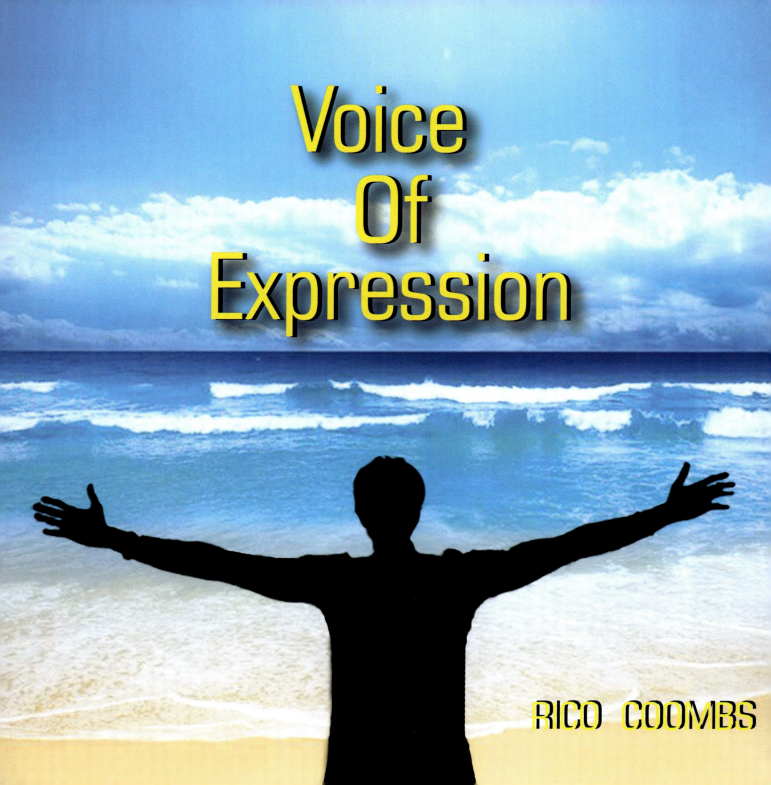

AuthorHouse™ UK
1663 Liberty Drive
Bloomington, IN 47403 USA
www.authorhouse.co.uk
UK TFN: 0800 0148641 (Toll Free inside the UK)
UK Local: 02036 956322 (+44 20 3695 6322 from outside the UK)

Because of the dynamic nature of the Internet, any web addresses or links contained in this book may have changed since publication and may no longer be valid. The views expressed in this work are solely those of the author and do not necessarily reflect the views of the publisher, and the publisher hereby disclaims any responsibility for them.

Any people depicted in stock imagery provided by Getty Images are models, and such images are being used for illustrative purposes only.
Certain stock imagery © Getty Images.

This book is printed on acid-free paper.

ISBN: 978-1-6655-9228-4 (sc)
ISBN: 978-1-6655-9227-7 (e)

Print information available on the last page.

Published by AuthorHouse 08/30/2021

authorHOUSE®

CONTENTS

INTRO

Voice of Expression….

My baby… the art form of my heart. People who know me very well…

never mind.

If you do **not** know me very well, then after reading this book you will get to deconstruct me and get closer to the core of who I am.

Let us get back to the introduction. People who know me very well have consistently asked me how my poetry is going; "do you have any new material", or "when are you coming out with your second book"?

I have come up with a whole heap of excuses as to why I have not come out with my second poetry book. Here are some of them:

I was not ready to come out with my second book, and I wanted to get a poetry manager so I can increase sales and do better than my first book. But the most honest reason has been that I fell out of love with the art form which has been consistent with me—through all my ups and downs, smiles and frowns.

I love my art form so much; it has shaped me and plays a major part in my life. But throughout the years, there have been moments, days, and months where I have refused to write and speak my voice through my pen and pad to express myself. Lack of direction, feeling stagnant, and self-doubt has kept me from moving forward in confidence.

However, through the challenges, poetry has been my refuge, my companion, soulmate, and a constant reminder of who I truly am. She is a partner who lets me express myself, have fun, be laid back, and take life in my stride.

Loyalty is an essential characteristic, and poetry has been loyal to me throughout my life's journey. So, I owe it to her to repay her and thank her for sticking by my side.

The first step to repaying her was to ink the title of one of my poems, "Talent *Inspires *Greatness," which is also in this book for you to enjoy.

The second step has been to create this poetic masterpiece called Voice of Expression, for you all to let it enter your mind, body and soul and to come along with me on a journey of expression.

So, sit back, relax, take life in your stride, and enjoy Rico Coombs' Voice of Expression.

DISCLAIMER

Where I'm From (my first poetry book) includes the poems: "Confession Part I," "II" and "III" and, you know, Usher did a Confession part IIII.

So, like Usher, I had to do it again, baby.

If you want to follow the story from the beginning, you can purchase *Where I'm From* and read all of the "Confessions" from the top.

I hear you all say, "that's great marketing," because you'll increase sales for your first poetry book, *Where I'm From*.

Rico Coombs

V OF E

I'm like an excited child,

My feelings can't be concealed.

I can't wait for all to be revealed: the surprise,

The suspense has all been anticipated,

I appreciate the time and patience you have shown while you have waited.

My life in words is between your fingertips,

I look forward to your views, opinions and critiques.

Be honest,

I won't feel offended if you think it's shit.

I hope I've done y'all justice,

I hope I've made y'all proud,

Voice of Expression,

This is my voice out loud.

VALERIE

I'm a household name;

Yet my art only appears in my house, not a gallery.

My art is old school, like the bold and curve blackberries.

I'll pause, and let that sink in.

But if you doubt my honesty, let's ask my friend from my Monoux days.

The one who was birthed called Valerie.

She was and still is amazed how I turn normal words into a colourful reality.

I'm honoured that she admires my artistry.

But I do doubt my capacity, which is the purity for my delay in my poetic variety.

AN INSIGHT TO ME

My bars are so phat, I guess I need lypo.

First time Sherene Jay heard Deep End; she said, Rico Coombs, you sound like a poetic pro.

Before my book was published, I was in financial deficit.

Now my talent is attracting increased attention; so fuck it, I can never quit.

I'm not a practising Christian, but in my first book, I mentioned Christ quite a bit.

But since my mother's death, the church we attended, I rarely visit.

I write poetry in my sleep; and the reason why I got into it is because I can't ride a beat.

My first introduction to poetry was when I was in school in Jamaica at the age of six.

When my schoolteachers use to give me licks in my hand middle with a bamboo stick.

When I came back to England, in the east side of London is where I spent most of my time.

Where prior to the Olympics employment opportunities was minimal all of the time.

That's why certain civilians enter the life of crime.

Some outsmart the system, whereas others push weights to pass the time.

Due to my upbringing, I became rooted like a sycamore tree.

But I'll let you into a little secret, once I contemplated selling Class B.

But now my objective is to graduate from university with a first-class honours degree

And motivate the younger generation to emulate me.

LION KING

I'm a LION KING

In search of my PRIDE

Call me SIMBA

In the JUNGLE, wandering ALONE

With no REFUGE as my HOME

Rico Coombs

Concrete Jungle 2017

Concrete jungle
But appreciate paradise.
White sand and tranquillity
It's a beautiful sight.

Hot days
Warm nights
That's the price you pay.
Once you catch a first class flight
Happy faces

Playful children of different races.
United together by the sun.
But separated by nationalities and birth places.

COLD DAYS / HOT NIGHTS

Cold days
Hot nights
First class flights
Is that a price?
Right.
To gain inspiration
To reflect and write an artistic compilation.
To create equality for ever colour, creed and nation
To create a picture
To make words into an imagery
To bring poetry to life and create an illustration.

Rico Coombs

J.A.M.A.I.C.A

J-uici beef patties

    A-ppleton estate

        M-anchester's Mandeville

      A-laine

        I-shawana

          C-ool runnings, peace be di journey

            A-Bog walk and Kingston's August Town

POETRY AND HENNESSEY

Poetry and Hennessey.

Blurred thoughts and distant memories.

Departure lounges.

New international territories.

Where my art form is duty free.

And the liquor is priced right.

Good vibes and positive energy.

Rico Coombs

TROPICAL PARADISE

They say beauty is in the eye of the beholder,

That's why I am beholding you.

Sun kissed skin

With melanin…

that's a chocolate delight.

Gazing smile,

Hair that when the wind goes by,

It flutters like a butterfly.

Eyes that twinkle in the night sky,

I call you my tropical paradise.

FR33LY

She is wintertime:

                                     Fine.

Topaz is her birthstone

A few months from now, we will be drinking cocktails by the coast.

While she admires the rural landscape

Of one of Africa's Capes,

Observing nature roaming freely in its habitat.

One shall be in his element

Watching the water channel into the harbour.

Nature taking its course

Shall ignite his creative floodgates to open.

To aid me to write international poetry freely.

Rico Coombs

NUBIAN EXCELLENCE

Shorty got arse,

Class and intellect;

She's a freedom fighter—call her a Suffragette.

She's a child of Destiny,

Maybe that's why I lose my breath.

She's the lead girl in retrospect.

She is from the borough where the Northerners

Think Wretch is the best.

Seaview

32:

One may define it as

Picturesque

She's an artistic piece.

With her,

More is less

She leaves me marvelled,

Like a cartoon sketch.

When her melanin.

Hits the canvas.

Call it,

Nubian Excellence.

Rico Coombs

INSPIRATIONAL QUEEN

International Women's Day.

So while my Queen is downstairs cooking I got to pay homage

to her struggle, her fights, her strengths and achievements.

You are a human like many women before you and after you, you have your faults.

But what attracts me to you is your strength from within.

Your fire,

Your passion

To make the world a better place.

Inspiring your fellow women of various shades and all races.

Reminding them that there are women to look up to.

You inspire them—whether they email, call, text or tell you face to face.

You also inspire me too.

That's why I Thank God every morning that I wake up next to your beautiful face.

-Mr Coombs

PACK OF CARDS

I'm the ace of SPADES,
But she sees me as a JOKER.
I'm her KING of the pack,
But she wants to be the QUEEN next to me
To reign supreme.
She claims she is the QUEEN of HEARTS
Yet I'm the creative type
Does this mean I'm the KING of ART?

Rico Coombs

OBSOLETE

Poetry is my passion

My heart and soul

But for a long time

I've been missing,

Reminiscing…

How I've forgotten to flirt

With my premonition.

I've been absent

One could say I've been obsolete

Now I've returned.

In summary I am back

It's not the return of Mark Morrison

Nor the return of 2pac

But I've returned from my cremation.

While y'all are sleeping, I'm up at my workstation

Illustrating and meditating

How I can make poetry fun

While teaching similes, metaphors, and alliterations

And how my dream is to get my poetry

Incorporated in English literature's poetic decoration

Thinking about my international aspiration for my art form

How my poetry can be involved in global migration and

international domination.

I Can't Stop

I can't stop writing poetry because it's a part of me, like my veins,

arteries, and my capillaries.

It's my world, my universe and my sphere.

A poem a day makes Rico's day, which is why my pen and pad are

always in close proximity.

I am addicted to it, like how a fean is addicted to his next hit.

Poetry is the one who I confide in at night, and we regularly converse up until morning light.

This is the only person I reveal my deepest and darkest thoughts to, just as the sun is on the horizon.

Poetry knows me inside out and knows the correct combination to decode me like a Rubik's cube.

When inspirational thoughts come into my head, poetry and I discuss and delegate what words will be written in black ink on my notepad.

I can't excommunicate myself from my beloved art form, as we are entwined like a woven tapestry.

If our connection or bond was ever broken, I would be confused, bewildered, and have no sense of direction.

My purpose in life would be pointless, because poetry completes me like how a full stop concludes a finished sentence.

Poetry is an essential part of my life, like how my melanin is a part of my dark chocolate skin; and how humanity is destined to sin.

I FLIRT

I flirt with poetry

I use it to express my INSECURITIES

I like to combine poetry and spoken word

I call it "POETIC UNITY"

Sincerely I do doubt my ABILITY

My CONTENT and its PURITY.

LACK OF...

I am my worst enemy
I am catastrophic
To my own downfall.
Class of 2012,
Yet others graduated with flying colours.
But I feel stagnant as Arsene Wenger's Arsenal.
Minimal accolades for my tireless and occasional sleepless nights.
I am my worst enemy,
The fire,
The flame,
The fight within me is now gone.
I need to ignite the flame.
Start back the fire,
Claim my rightful
Crown,
Position
And reign supreme at the top.

MY LIFE IS A STORY BOOK

My life is a story book

For all to see.

Some have already completed it,

While others are on the first chapter.

Individual's read through the ink

Which I have penned onto a selection of white sheets of paper.

PAUSE

Through this, readers have the opportunity of seeing life through my eyes.

Words and sentences which I would never speak out in public

Are written down and visible for all to see.

It's amazing, how an emotionless person can display his full emotions from his pen...

In the world of adjectives and nouns,

My secrets are no longer safe; and I feel completely exposed.

I am not ashamed or embarrassed, about what I have revealed.

It's just an opportunity to get to know me on a deeper

and personal level.

I hope through this book I have answered all the pondering questions you wanted to ask me,

But were afraid to approach me and ask me personally.
That's the entire preliminary taken care of so...
Welcome to voice of expression where all is revealed.
Just like a streaker running awol on a football field.

SOMETIMES

Sometimes I wonder why people like me.

I'm just a normal individual who writes poetry.

All I do is write poetry in my sleep and hope one day I can master riding a beat.

People say I'm an inspiration to many; just because of the way that I write; and how my poetic charisma caresses the mic.

I don't write poetry for the fame, or the material gain.

Just to make family and friends be proud to hear Rico Coombs' first and last name.

I write about a variety of things, whether it's from adidas to palm trees, or deep end and the boisterous seas.

I was gifted with this talent six years after birth and this art form has defined what my purpose is on this earth.

Certain people noticed my talent from the get-go; and I'm getting increased attention, which is why I have to copyright my poetic flow.

I'm just amazed how people love my form of art; just because I write about issues close to my heart.

I'm humbled by the positive responses people say.

A smile always comes to my face when people say my poetry has impacted them in a unique and special way.

Just hearing those words helps improve my day.

I'll be honest I never knew my parker pen would take me this far.

PAUSE

Thank you to all the people who supported me through my poetry journey, and I hope you sit back and enjoy this collaboration book.

ACUTE ANGLE

I'm thinking about life from a different angle.

Acute to be precise.

Wondering how I can make my dreams INTO reality;

While still trying to minimise the risk of fatality.

Stressing my brain, trying to think: and now it's keeping me up

PAUSE

I'm currently enduring sleepless nights: which is why I never sleep a wink.

Heavy eyed; I look like a zombie.

You could call me the living dead.

All I need is a coffin and a tombstone..... to confirm I am officially dead.

Tunnel vision to achieve my destiny

Yet still envy is trying to jealous me.

PAUSE

They say keep your enemies close and your friends closer..... When you're turning your dreams into reality.

This is why my eyes are fixated on my friends......

And my enemies are in my peripherals.... so neither of them is out of sight

PAUSE

I am vigilant of their every move.

I am focused....

Like a Ford; and connected to success, like how Rico Coombs was connected to his mother via her umbilical cord.

PAUSE

I know I can achieve my objectives, but obstacles are in my way.

Rocks and boulders are coming down towards me..... on this uphill struggle of success.

I am destined for success: and I will succeed.

So that I can reflect back on my experiences and memories as inspiration

Whenever I am deflated.... on the road to success.

INSOMNIA

3 o'clock starts or anytime after that

Is the normal time I arise up from my slumber.

Caption that

It's a regular occurrence regardless of whether

It's a weekday or weekend

Showing no regards for my employment calendar.

Yet it messes with a man's pay.

A lot is on my mind

Rethinking

Forward thinking

And playing out scenarios in my head.

Which have me perplexed and confused

Thinking of methods

To change the current and future situations,

The outcome and my future mood,

Situations which are on my mind and so dear to my heart.

THE ROAD TO SUCCESS KNOWS NO DAYS OFF

The road to success knows no days off...

So don't be surprised... if sleepless nights are the price I pay at the toll booth.

Regularly I am up writing poetry... so I guess you can it overtime.

When the city is asleep, poetically that is when I come alive.

ROCKING

I pray for the DEMONS that watch over me.

I try to flee them, but they are continuously…

troubling my soul.

Rocking back and forth,

A figurative in my mind…

but secured in my moral flesh.

Cracks are visible,

But…

I can't be a weak link in the CHAIN.

I gotta carry on the vision.

The LEGACY,

The dynasty is in the palm of my hands.

EMULATE ME

People want to emulate me, but I stay rooted like a sycamore tree.

Some teachers said I was going to fail, but look at me now, I have prevailed.

I've made it through hard times, sunshine and rain; I'm still flying high like an aeroplane.

Within myself I have believed and look at me now, I am reaping the benefits which I have achieved.

Life is a journey, life is a race, but I'm holding it down at a steady pace.

I'm focused like a Ford and I'm connected to success like how a baby is connected to its mother via the umbilical cord.

There is only one of me, I'm unique, different, and distinct. You know what makes me special because I stand out like the colour pink.

I'm proud of what I have achieved in life: even through all the pain and strife.

I put my heart and my soul into what I write, and I'm holding it down and I'm keeping it tight.

Don't follow me or try to emulate me, because you know what, I'm just doing me.

INSPIRATION

Inspired by the hills and the greenery.

While the sun is beating down on my melanin skin.

The scenery of the hill looks

Picturesque.

Words can't begin to describe what my eyes are currently taking in,

Driving above the speed limit to get to our destination.

Music on blast

While she jiggling that arse... in the driver's seat.

California casual is the attire of the day.

Heading to be one with nature,

One with the sea.

FREEDOM

The freedom of writing is like freedom of speech,

Having the freedom to speak what comes to mind

Without any restriction,

Compromise; and with conviction,

Speaking whatever comes to your mind via your heart

Freedom to educate like a teacher

Preach like a preacher and motivate like a speaker

The freedom to be oneself.

CAPTURING MEMORIES

Holding hands while at Gatwick Airport, skimming stones while sunbathing on Icelmer Beach.

Admiring artwork at Saatchi and Saatchi, followed by amazing London beauty from up in the sky.

Dinners and cocktails, YumYum and Mem and Laz are definitely two of our favourite spots.

Ice skating and driving a car on Ally Pally's Lake.

All the memories I'll treasure, as the weekends and months continue onto another anniversary.

Let's continue to capture our memories and continue to build more.

WEST INDIES POETRY

I'm writing poetry in the West In-dies

Or the Maldives,

Palm trees.

This is when I am liberated and poetically free…to incapacitate and articulate.

Sweet scents of elegance.

While I observed the daily activities of the residents.

When I'm around nature,

I'm in my element….

I feel as I am at the pinnacle.

I feel like a POETIC PRESIDENT.

SUN KISSED

They say I'm sun-kissed.

Touched with heavenly RAYS.

As my complexion is my complimented by our source of life.

When the humidity blends in with my melanin skin.

Beaming with elegance,

Courteous of the British summer.

WINTER WONDERLAND

I wake up from my winter slumber and open my curtains, to be greeted by Jack Frost.

I put on my numerous layers and begin to brave the cold.

Winter is here and I can feel the cold Arctic wind caressing my face.

My hands become numb and my eyes water, due to the freezing temperature.

The intensity of the cold wind makes me feel as though I have put my head into an igloo.

The temperature is below zero, yet still no snow is visible on the horizon.

Weather warnings have been repeatedly enforced by weather experts.

The vigorous strength of the wind is swaying the trees from… side to side.

Now I am safely inside, I am wrapped up warm, drinking my hot cup of cocoa and watching the snow settle all over the pavement.

I see children and grown-ups making snowmen and star angels, decorating this vast winter savannah.

Footprints and car tyres are imprinted in the snow as people commute to and from their various destinations.

Outside looks like a winter blanket and is a winter wonderland for everyone to enjoy.

The trickling snow is settling on stationary cars and on residential buildings.

Welcome to my winter wonderland of March 2013.

Rico Coombs

BRITISH WEATHER

In my Russian hat, and my favourite white winter coat…

adapting to this winter cold.

Don't be surprised if we experience snow

In Euston Square.

I wish I was there; bring me back to….

the island of sunshine.

Where my melanin skin absorbs the sunlight.

Yet I'm in an icebox

I am in need of some sunshine.

One may call it vitamin D

I'mmmmm on… Anti-freeze as… blue blood is pumping

Through my veins, arteries, and capillaries.

Cold air.

Escapes via my Icelandic lips; my lips are sealed.

They're frozen solid

With a touch of frost, the word COLD

Is an understatement

Yet I am not over exaggerating

I'm just currently stating that…

Rico Coombs

WISH YOU WERE HERE

Wish you were here

or

bring me back to…

Is a common cry from numerous people.

They seek stimulation and satisfaction

From jet set holidays abroad.

Snapchat and Instagram,

displays and records the picturesque scenery…

while highlighting their adventures.

Is this a cry for help?

A state of depression…

oppression of the mind…

Masking their true feelings from within.

Thrill seeking for the mere moment,

But depressed in their everyday routine.

Bored of their consistency,

Yet they have stagnated their growth.

But look for holidays as an escape,

But one which is temporary,

Three weeks to be precise.

A change of routine,

Instead of change of scenery,

Might just be the recipe

Or the remedy,

even the resolution

To conclude

Their state of depression of their own reality.

We are in charge of our destiny.

Change your current situation

And create your actual reality.

Rico Coombs

CARIBBEAN LOVER

They asked me what makes me happy.

I tell them I'm aroused by my baby's intellect.

Some may call it foreplay.

I assure you..

You haven't seen nothing yet.

She is my Coco Cabana,

My Caribbean lover.

I need her like Cuba needs Havana,

Like Barbados needs Rihanna.

The sight of her …inspires ME like no other.

Words can't come from my mouth,

I stutter.

My love, my friend,

My love for her knows no end.

Around her my mind gets erected;

We are entwined we are connected

I go bareback with her, but I'm protected.

She injects my mind....

And let's me look at life from a different perspective.

Honestly, I should spend more time with her,

Yet with her at times I'm withdrawn,

But luckily, she never tells me

She feels neglected.

You are my blessing,

You are my heaven,

That's why I'm voicing my expression.

My love

My all

Poetically for you I fall.

SCIENCE

You are my science.

When our lips entwine and our saliva exchange,

I can see chemistry…

When we meet, biologically our bodies speak.

You are my physics, which is why we are physically attracted to one another

Your sweet scent of excellence is my favourite aroma.

Your intellect arouses me, when I rise from my slumber.

JAMAICAN GIRL

I had a Jamaican girl who used to cook me ackee and saltfish with rundown.

Now she just wants to give me beans and toast and jacket potatoes.

Occasionally if I am in luck I might get cod and chips.

I guess she's become to westernise and feels like I am an English man.

I may be born and raised in Hackney but I assure you I can still twang.

I need my yam, dumpling and green banana, that's what I am used to eating because it sustains me for the whole day.

Just because I reside in the British capital does not mean that my cultural food cannot be part of my diet.

Well, if a little yam is good for the Jamaican athletes, then I am sure it is good enough for me.

Well maybe as she is classified as a British citizen, now she believes it is acceptable to throw the Jamaican cuisine outta door.

If she wants to continue this relationship, she needs to be filling my belly with that traditional hard food.

If she does not, then boy, I am not responsible for my actions.

Because I really need me a Jamaican Girl.

İÇMELER BEACH

As far as the human eye can see....

green mountain tops united by the İçmeler sea.

The tide is slowly washing the salty water to shore.

Tranquil and heavenly is how I feel while writing this piece of art.

With my girlfriend by my side..... goldenly kissed by the sun's rays.

Reading her exotic collection of literature.

Continental music echoing across the beach.

The sun is beginning to descend on the horizon.

Boats are beginning to leave the shore for their sunset cruises.

Locals and tourists invite us for photos......

and together we share a bowl of fruit and cocktails.

My girlfriend decides to take a break from reading.

She takes me by the hand; and we walk entwined until the sand and sea meet.

Together we skim flat stones across the water.

Today's motto is:
ONE WITH LIFE & ONE WITH NATURE!!!

Palm trees swaying from side to side; orchestrated under their own accord.

Next to us the pier, has been stripped naked of its sun beds and ashtrays

Tables and chairs are being carried out for dinner under the moonlight.

Classical music begins to play…. while the water relays back and forth from the shore.

Entering customers are invited to take their seats and observe the beautiful surroundings.

Complimentary champagne has been poured out, and it has now been distributed to the seated customers.

Welcome to İçmeler, a popular Turkish tourist destination.

Time is of the Essence

I'm on time for planes, trains and online video games.

But late for… mates and dinner dates,

I'll confess I've made a few girls wait as well.

But it's not my typical tradition,

I promise, please… listen.

It's not a reoccurrence,

It's just coincidence,

Please accept my apology.

I know I'm late to meet you, that's why I'm calling.

Two days after Monday morning,

I apologise with sincerity;

I'm working to make this a rarity.

Are you surprised your apologies regularly go on deaf ears?

Rico, it's like you're blind… to the fact that your timekeeping is whack.

Even evident as you still try to fight back.

Truly, I'm sorry, you're right and I'm wrong.

"Is it too late to say I'm sorry?"

Has now officially become our theme song.

TRUST ISSUES

Trust issues:

I never trust a woman with a wedding band

Because she has other plans.

This isn't a confession;

I guess you could call it the truth.

> I could see it in her eyes.
> "Boy, you're cute."
> You should see her intense stare.
> While she twirls and plays with her extended hair.

When the cat is away, the mouse is at play.

She vowed she would stay on the straight and narrow... but now diverting…

at the next intersection.

> Is it ironic that we crossed paths in the hallway?
> Her wink
> Gives me the impression
> She is willing to stray.

He is none the wiser.

That I'm his wife's secret admirer.

While he is building the empire,

She is tearing it apart.

Now you know why I'm single and a female has never claimed my heart.

This is my confession
On a Friday night
In May
Live from London's Archway.

Rico Coombs

NUDE

Reminiscing

On the premonition

Of us kissing

Has me missing

When you wore no makeup

And were bare…

Nude down to the toes and fingernails

Is the colour

Which I really like

Yet you prefer

The multi-coloured

Approach

Was it because of the attention

Or was it just your intended selection.

SUSPICION

She wants me to confess

But for her request I reject,

Deflecting the conversation.

I guess you could call that the art of how to digress.

She wants me to give her my all.

But honestly at the beginning I was putting in less.

If you ask her, she would tell you she suspected.

Her uncertainty…

made her question my honestly and integrity.

I have created a ruin, and everything is turning into debris.

Triggering her female intuition,

Getting hints and finding clues

On a conquest to apprehend.

But she would never let no one challenge her authority, or de-throne her position.

A Queen who reigns SUPREME and who is TRUE 2 HER RELIGION.

CONFESSION (EXTENDED) PART IIII

My man and I broke up.

But I've liked you from the get-go.

Your intellectual conversation and muscles caught my attention, but I was attracted to your eyes the most.

Your smile and your laughter had me at hello.

A shoulder to lean on, someone who always listens to what I say and whom I can confide in.

PAUSE

I've always liked you, but I've been in a committed relationship for a while and I honoured the union.

Although I did contemplate pursuing.

When our eyes cross paths, I wonder if we were destined to be friends or something more.

I would definitely prefer the latter; but my heart is in a state of indecision.

When I needed him the most, he wasn't there for me;

Whereas you was!

There was always an excuse or explanation for his absence which falls on deaf ears.

A gap;

and a void was always there, but without knowing, you automatically filled it.

I wish I had you for myself (maybe I do but I just don't realise it).

I think about you when I'm with him; is that right? Lusting and lingering thoughts keep running through the corridors of my mind, while resting my eyes in bed.

I'm fighting temptations but honestly, I believe my emotions are starting to give in.

Is it right for me to feel this way; are my feelings for him really starting to rapidly deteriorate and decay?

Should I ever tell him the way I really feel or bottle it up and carry on normally?

This decision continuously puzzles my conscience and regularly I lose sleep over it.

LENGTHY PAUSE

Mirror, Mirror,

I'm torn between the two.

How should I decide my future, how should I decide my fate?

EMOTIONALLY DRAINED

Emotionally drained,

taking everything in like a sponge.

The wine makes me feel like I'm drowning,

and numb to the world.

Blocking out the guilt which I felt for the past.

While listening to her talk about her past.

I want to help, but I feel like all help and hope is gone.

I no longer can rescue this damsel in distress and save her from reality.

My superpowers have been retracted.

Yet my human frustration is visible.

I've been at this checkpoint numerous times before.

But will my guilt get the better of me

And will I go against my moral judgment?

UNSHACKLED

Cut loose, unshackled, unchained.

Feeling free, I can breathe once again.

I felt suffocated, as though I was straining myself.

Untrue to myself and my identity.

This isn't me, but I conformed to this, to be a people pleaser, yet still my needs have been neglected and swept underneath the carpet.

DECEIVED AND TRICKED

Deceived and tricked.

You're not the person I thought I knew.

Hiding behind a mask; and now all the cracks are visible for all to see.

You lying and deceitful little wretch, I trusted you.

But for my trust, all I received in return was grief, heartache, misery, and pain.

I thought blood was thicker than water; maybe, just maybe, it might be vice versa.

I feel down and out, vulnerable because you took advantage of me, but I was too blind to see.

Now I'm paying a lifelong penalty, for something you were too coward to admit.

Life is sweet and dandy for you, while my life is now a bed of thorns.

ALONE WITH MY THOUGHTS

Alone with my thoughts and no distractions.

Solitary confinement is what I need, and what I tell myself I desire.

Time to focus on myself and unwind.

Being around certain individuals makes my blood boil, but yet still I keep my mouth closed and have a cool and calm Coombs exterior.

Thoughts, stresses, and strains are pulsating on my cranium.

I need to distance myself fast and rapidly because my mental state is currently at STAKE.

There is only one thing I can confide to in solitary, and it gives me a sense of comfort and relief.

Which is why I pour myself out on my notepad via my beloved art form.

Tomorrow isn't promised

Tomorrow isn't promised, so make the most of today.

Because you don't know what the future holds.

Tell your nearest and dearest how much you love and appreciate them, and the value which they bring to your life.

Turn your dreams into reality.

So you can say you have accomplished the unthinkable.

Do something out of the ordinary; something crazy, spontaneous and fun.

So you can treasure those memories for life.

Spend time self-indulging and appreciating your self-worth.

Sadly, a lot of times people give so much of themselves to others and neglect their own selves.

Sometimes, you have to lock yourself off from others and give yourself time alone from the world.

Use this time to enhance your skills, hobbies and talents.

Love life, because you only live it once.

Because life has no pause, stop or rewind buttons; always remember that.

Be free,

Be at peace,

And be one with nature.

Because tomorrow isn't promised.

Rico Coombs

KEZIAH AND LATARA

It hurts me that I never saw Keziah and LaTara grow up.

I was never there to interrogate their first boyfriends, let alone see their first steps.

Sometimes I feel like I have failed my role as an older cousin.

The Atlantic Sea has separated us all from having a physical connection.

I've had to settle for phone conversations and internet interaction.

They currently reside in the land of the brave and the home of the free.

While I live in the country, where Elizabeth is the reigning monarchy.

I'm proud they are excelling in school and also at track and field.

I want you girls to always remember I love you both to bits,

Continue to grow into beautiful and responsible young ladies.

Love, your older cousin.
X

I HAVEN'T GIVEN UP

Don't think I've given up on you.

Just because I've been absent,

Doesn't mean I don't care about you.

Nor does that mean you aren't close to my heart.

I vowed that I'll never leave you nor forsake you.

Although I'm not ever present,

I'm watching you from a distance,

Just know that that you are well protected and incredibly well-loved.

Never forget that,

Keep those words close to your heart.

Because
YOU'RE WISE
YOU'RE SPECIAL
AND YOU'RE WONDERFUL.

INNER ME

I hope they don't think….

because I don't ring them often that I do not love them.

If my heart could speak to them,

They could see my true feelings,

The true me.

Sometimes I feel that their mistakes in life are a result of me.

I beat myself up frequently,

that I should be there, to be a better role model and uphold my responsibilities.

Honestly, I am proud of both of you…

although I may not say it regularly.

Distance shouldn't be an excuse,

but it plays a role…

in our separation.

I pray that you have used my absence to your advantage.

That you both have used it as a learning curve.

Sometimes I ponder,

Would both of them have learnt those life lessons if I was present,

or would I have tried to protect them from what life has in store for them?

I guess that's the past,

That's why it's called history.

That's why from now on,

It will be history that I am not present

In their future.

MISS BROWN

Granny says I don't ring her digits;

I guess she is missing me.

7 weeks in Jamaica;

I guess my presence was a present,

minus the Christmas tree.

She says she looks up to me,

yet she is the pinnacle of the family tree,

and the creator of this dynamic dynasty.

I love her unconditionally,

which is why she is included as part of my responsibilities.

I'm just repeating history as she did that for me,

from infancy.

Miss Brown told me

I can achieve anything in life, by applying my full ability.

If I did,

I would be lethal

With my poetic poetry.

But she worries that my stubbornness and ignorance will hinder me,

And doesn't want me to turn dark,

Like my skin colour in humidity…

when it is exposed to vitamin D.

Rico Coombs

POET'S CARNA

Poet's carna…

English is rolling up di marijuana.

                                               PAUSE

Dear Fada, please look after Grandma…

She is my responsibility.

That's why I grind a little harder

The same way I'm responsible for the little one

Who calls me Fada

I'm a bastard

PAUSE

Let's blank out that bit about my Fada

                                               PAUSE

While we pay our respect to Naiylah grandma

A Strong Black Woman

A definition of a strong black woman is someone who, in the absence of her children's father, can raise her children on her own.

Don't get me wrong; I'm not saying that a single mother summarises a definition of a strong black woman.

I'm just showing recognition for their efforts which normally go in vain.

This is a person who can make a negative situation into a positive one, with limited resources.

A strong black woman is someone, who works hard during the day, but still makes time to spend with her offspring.

True strong black women have to be commended as they have to endure numerous trials and tribulations.

The trials and tribulations which she experiences only make her stronger and wiser.

A strong black woman is the foundation of the black community.

Without her existence, I assure you that people that share the same skin colour as me and you would be extinct just like the Australian dodo bird.

They say the hand that rocks the cradle rocks the world, and the cradle is still rocking due to her steady hand.

A black woman is a lady who takes no crap; and uses disciplinary methods to keep her children in check and in line.

This is a woman who is not afraid of using the belt, as she believes the ethos, don't spear the rod and spoil the child.

She believes it is better that she beats her children, with love and care than when police brutally assault them.

A true strong black lady is someone who paves the way so that their children can be successful, and also warns them to be selective of the company which they keep.

A woman who teaches her children to be domesticated, which means to cook, clean, wash and iron.

The reason for this is because she does not want her children to depend on no one.

A true strong black woman does not let things get to her, and just carries on treading life's journey.

She is a queen who reigns supreme with love, compassion and order, who wants to see her children succeed and make the most out of life.

A MOTHER'S LOVE; WHICH SHE NEVER HAD

All she wanted was to be loved by the lady, who brought her into this world.

She never understood why her mother, never loved and appreciated her.

Her endless endeavours to feel her mother's warm embrace and words of encouragement came to no avail.

When she used to cry, her mother's hands were never there to comfort her or dry her tearful eyes.

She faced the world alone; and she never had a comforting blanket to shelter her from life's turbulent storms.

Whenever her friends spoke about their mothers, she just hung her head down in shame.

She never understood why her mother never loved her, and to this day, this question is unanswered.

Her mother is a stranger to her; and is more concerned about other individuals whose DNA and chromosomes differ from her own.

Imagine a lady who is always willing to help others, but never willing to look after her number one responsibility.

Yet her daughter still never had a bad word to utter against the lady who delivered her into this world.

Will this lady ever love her daughter? This is a question which regularly puzzles many.

Can the experience of her growing up without her mother make this woman a stronger person?

Or will it affect her when she has her first born?

PAUSE

Only time will tell.

BUILDER MAN

I carry a chip on my shoulder like a builder man.

Leonard was her father, he was a builder man.

Flight's been booked to Jamaica, the destination.

A few weeks later organising a funeral wasn't the ideal plan.

From a boy to a man was the transition.

Making her proud is my ultimate mission,

Reminiscing… that I'm missing her while listening to her favourite song.

Laid her to rest in her mother's land.

She grew up in Tottenham, but never was a fan.

But Arsenal's Ian Wright was her main man.

CHRISTIAN

I was brought up in a Christian household.

But I'm not a practising Christian.

Yet still I recite a few passages of scripture.

PAUSE

I do believe in Christ.

So constantly I ask Jesus to walk with me, like how he accompanied Kanye.

I wouldn't class myself as religious, but I definitely keep the Lord in the picture.

Am I a hypocrite, because when times are rough, I fall on my knees and pray for help support and guidance through whatever situation I am facing?

Or is that in fact.... human nature… to seek divine intervention when stuff are not always going our way.

PAUSE

When I was a child, I was eager and excited to go to church.

Now, as an adult, I come up with every excuse for why I can't attend church on a Saturday.

To be honest, I can't tell the last I prayed.

I beg your pardon; I did recite a few lines while departing London Gatwick's runway.

Would you be surprised if I confessed sending a few words heavenwards before arriving at my last international destination?

My grandma always reminds me to read my psalms and have a daily dialogue with the Lord.

To be truthful, I do find it hard to have a dialogue with a guy who doesn't reply via verbal response.

I always find it ironic that…

I'm always nudged to bless the dinner table.

PAUSE

I guess this Christmas it will not be any different.

ROLE MODEL

There is only one male role model

I look up to.

So, this poem is overdue.

Regardless of your adversities, you pull

Through.

If I was in your shoes,

I don't know if I would have pulled through.

Even though regularly, you are in different countries

Around the world,

You make sure we stay connected

Via skype

Imo

Facebook

Or telephone.

We find any form of connection.

Irrespective.

I remember our conversations listening to:

music, swigging our liquor.

While writing on the train

I feel quite reflective.

Our talks about life, certain images for me were blurred.

You helped me to paint a clear picture;

you have love in your heart;

honestly I don't know how

You do it.

I wouldn't do what you did.

But you laid it all "two" rest.

That's why this poem is overdue.

Alexander the Great

Reigning King supreme

The God of his palace

A supernatural human being

BRUVA FROM ANOTHER

I have the utmost respect for you, bro.
Only a few people have seen me bare.
RAW to the CORE
You knew me in my "TRUEST AND REALEST" form.
When I was wandering through my personal wilderness,
You helped me through my traumatic storm.
An aid
A rescue
A lifeboat
In the treacherous waters.

TOGETHER WE WILL PULL THROUGH

It's been a difficult road and there are some words which I regret ever uttering out of my mouth.

It's been a rollercoaster ride and the horror journey is still continuing.

They say what doesn't kill you, makes you stronger.

In our case it just seems to be drifting us apart.

It's been taking its toll on us physically and mentally and our happy faces have turned to permanent scowls.

I wish this sad and dark period will end and a brighter day and a new dawn will begin.

I lay it all down at the feet of the almighty; I've even asked for divine intervention to guide and protect us, and to give us the strength to pull through.

I'm sorry you had to go through this.

I thank you and am grateful for your support and strength.

May this just be a minor blip in our long and fruitful relationship.

May the sunshine on us again and remove this dark and grey cloud of gloom.

THERE IS NOTHING LIKE MY BED

The obsession

Infatuation

I have for the object…

Which I lay my head on… and which cradles me to sleep is…. priceless.

The way she curves to my skin and my bedsheets,

which are soft linen.

She knows my every curve and bump,

as I manoeuvre into my final resting place for the night.

They say sleep is the cousin of death.

And when I'm asleep, I'm dead as a door knob.

Quiet as a church mouse.

I sleep peacefully like a child who has just been breastfed.

My sleep is peaceful,

my sleep is tranquil.

It's heavenly,

as my eyes slowly

shift side to side.

I yawn,

and my weary head

crashes on my pillow,

Like an avalanche coming to an abrupt halt.

Sleep is on my horizon.

TURBULENCE

I feel her pain, which is why I can sympathise with what she is going through.

No one should feel that anguish and pain, but life is cruel.

Which is why you have to take what you are going through with a pinch of salt.

I guess when you go upstairs you can ask the creator why bad things happen to good people.

Life is unfair but you have to ride through it to complete the complex course.

Individually we are different, but collectively, we have the same thoughts.

You are a strong individual who has come a long way.

Many would be bewildered and confused if they were in your shoes.

You are a lighthouse and a beacon of hope for people who will one day go through your situation.

No one knows your pain, but I can promise you that the sun will shine through the rain.

You are an inspiration, but I am sure you don't even know it.

My thoughts are with you even though you are millions of miles away at sea.

HEART SONG

Death is only a heartbeat away…

But for some it's only a few feet away.

Let me invite you into Vanessa's world…

Her father's Golden Girl,

The apple of her daddy's eyes.

But she is hurting inside and feels there's no one to confide in.

Reckless nights and dragging days.

She wants the nights to end,

But dreads the day when his body becomes…

ice cold and his soul shall ascend.

Feeling trapped, bewildered, and confused.

Accepting something which she has no control over or no choice.

She wants answers but who can she question.

Mentally she is accepting what's happening…

yet physically she cannot connect.

In a reflective mood…

she drifts into a happy place, filled with treasured memories.

PAUSE

It's destiny

Its fate

She prays that God will withhold his arrival to those eternal pearly gates.

COUSIN OF DEATH

They say sleep is the cousin of death, which is why she does not want to go into a deep coma.

She is fighting it, but her mind over matter strategy is just not working.

Her eyelids are feeling heavy and she is fighting for the sunshine to penetrate through her iris.

Vaguely, she can see a masculine figure with a white robe stretching out both of his hands.

Her family huddle around her bedside, linking their hands together praying to the Almighty.

Right now, she's inhaling and exhaling deep breaths, and she starts to shiver.

She is looking pale, and the melanin is being sucked from her skin.

Her heartbeat is fluctuating on the hospital apparatus.

Finally, the apparatus makes a lengthy beep throughout the ward, and down the corridor.

Her breath gracefully leaves her body and evaporates into the atmosphere.

Now her spirit evaporates into a white dove and flies away through the hospital.

The nursing staff try to console her mourning family, but words of condolences are meaningless.

Rico Coombs

KING'S ROAD

A little piece of heaven on my left breast;

What's a Lion King, without his Lion Queen?

Always full of joy, laughter and passion,

my trophy piece,

always success driven.

There's a dark side, with abuse and racism.

It's a domestic issue, which is swept under the carpet.

Dirty laundry, that should be dealt with at home,

Get spilt onto the King's Road.

The road… where King's rode… celebrating victories and champion "Knights."

The world sees the good, bad and our ugly.

honestly, I'm ashamed of our past, but optimistic about a positive future.

But we have got to address the elephant in the room.

Verbal and physical abuse, but yet we stand hand in hand.

Kicking, spitting and punching.

Hurtful things are said and it messes with my mental core.

People say we are not destined to be,

But you can't choose who you love.

She chose me.

Chelsea FC

PEACE

All I ever wanted was my soul and my peace

No justice no peace

They crucify me, because I missed from the spot.

They tell me loosen up, but they have their pitch forks and nooses up

Three Lions, in the UK.

In the Union jack we trust

With the three lions, they glorify the beast from Africa…

but within these times… they cage me up like a beast from Africa.

Embracing my cuisine and culture.

But circling vultures trying to attack these… Lion Kings and try to dismantle my pride.

2021 but feels like the dark ages, this is going on for ages… but now it's on the front pages.

Windrush generation was given the green light to enter Britain's shores,

but now they are showing us the door and telling us to close it behind us.

We have overstayed our welcome and we are no longer welcomed here.

TALENT INSPIRES GREATNESS- THE LEGACY

Talent inspires greatness. Which is why Malcolm X, Marcus Messiah Garvey and Nelson Mandela motivate me.

They inspire me to achieve my potential… and never give up in the face of adversity.

These individuals paved the way for me to be bold, stand up tall and strong.

Their impact changed, the dynamics in the century in which I was conceived.

Their fight, grit and determination is something I wish I could have inherited; even if it's an ounce of what they all possessed.

Men of great prestige and power, fighting for the cause of justice.

So that individuals can be liberated and have a freedom of expression.

Remembered for their individual… and collective changes in society and throughout this century.

They spoke… and believed the truth and inspired others also to believe; even in the face of hate and adversity.

They continued to fly the flag of truth at full mast.

Whether past, present or future, their legacies shall live on.

THE LIGHT

You are my salvation

You are my light

You believe in my ability…

And inspire me to write

You are the calm to my storm

You neutralise my wrath

It's been a long and winding road

But you are about to make it a clear path.

Thorns and thistles…

Wounds obtained from the blisters.

By battle scars, which are visible on both hands

It's a battlefield and numerous times

I want to fly the flag at half mask.

Yet you keep me

Rico Coombs

Focused and connected,

Although I have been

Derailed and disconnected,

Poetically I have neglected

My art form in retrospective.

SOMETIMES (REFIX)

Sometimes I feel lost in my own maze.
Sometimes I stutter and even forget my words on stage.
Sometimes my mind goes blank and nothing appears on my page.
Sometimes I feel like I've let my fans down and I'm ashamed.
Sometimes I am actually the one to blame.
But dwelling on the past, what will that change?

THE LIFE OF A STUTTERER

Spit it out; is what people use to say.

Why you thinking so much—about the next word to say.

I knew the words which I wanted to say but they just never wanted to come out.

People would regularly interrupt my sentences and say words of their own.

PAUSE

In my head, I always used to say: I don't need assistance, support or suggestions to finish my sentences off.

But people, please be patient with me until the words come out.

My words used to be rushed so I could avoid stammering.

It didn't help the situation, as I still stumbled upon the same problems.

My stammering use to commence when I had to speak in places full of people, and when asking for directions if I was lost.

Or speaking to the shop keeper, or the driver on the 253 bus.

I wish it could go away. It makes communication with people difficult, it just became a living hell.

Speech therapy and interacting with fellow stammerers helped me a lot and built up my confidence to speak out loud.

PAUSE

It still affects me now from time to time but I can handle it better now;

Years down the line.

Thank you for taking time to listen.

Next time you meet someone who finds it hard to speak;

Give them extra time and don't interject when they are trying to speak.

Rico Coombs

WRITER'S BLOCK

Some people say, "you write a lot."

I guess they would be astonished that even I experience writer's block.

My mind can be confused and perplexed.

At times it can bewildering

That I struggle to put words together into a creative format.

To write about a topic compelling to one's ear,

Or one that pulls on their heart strings…

Like a quartet.

I regularly beat myself up

If days pass when my pen and pad don't meet.

I feel curse and sometimes even sacrifice sleep.

But when I'm a free spirit, that's when my poetry comes alive.

Like a contagious infection

Its spreads like wildfire.

It's like a dragon,

Has been unleashed.

And

I call it di poetic beast.

PAUSE

Which gives me inner peace.

PURPOSE IN LIFE

I guess some point within our life expectancy, we question ourselves about what our purpose of life is.

For me, that thought frequently runs through the corridors of my cranium, so I guess I'm no different from the general population.

Numerous individuals say I am an individual, who is an inspiration and motivation to a vast congregation, yet still I question my ability.

I just push myself to the extreme boundaries, to obtain success and settle for nothing less, so I can make the lady who carried me for nine months proud, in her absence.

The trials and tribulations in my life have curved and moulded me into an individual who uses my personal experiences as a testimony to both the young and old.

Is my objective in life to be a successful black entrepreneur with a six-figure sum, or to convince young people not to be in possession of a metallic weapon called the gun?

Or is my purpose in life to touch the hearts of many, through my charismatic poetry?

People are amazed by my perseveration and dedication, and say I am multi-talented individual, so I have no limitations.

Is it because, in the face of adversity, I have not thrown in the towel or stumbled at life's first hurdle?

All I want to do is obtain my BA degree and hope the younger generation emulate me; and to build and empower my community, to live in peace and harmony.

Sitting down and pondering my purpose in life, while my feet are being massaged by the Caribbean sand.

I think I have just stumbled across the purpose of my life.

Poetic Masterpiece

Poetry is mine;

So, lyrically who can compete with me?

I'm making my dreams a reality...

Literally!

I love when my pen and pad are combined, I call it poetic harmony.

PAUSE

Previously, before my publication,

I used to perform voluntary...

But now for my lyrical content... individuals have to pay me a performance fee.

PAUSE

I'm free to express myself whether it's acapella or off-beat.

PAUSE

Poetry is my foundation, which is why my LOVE FOR HER IS CONCRETE.

My dedication and hard work is starting to pay off;

Which is why... I can see the royalties increase in my bank account.

PAUSE

My interest is growing around the world... this is why for my art form

... Foreign currencies are currently being accepted.

PAUSE

Global exposure was never my intention, but it's humbling that internationally individuals know my name.

Just because of my words, rhythm, and word play....

PAUSE

Now individuals want my poetry to symphonize...... with their music and create a musical melody.

When I am in the booth.... the combination sounds epic.... nah scrap that,

It sounds heavenly.

PAUSE

My art form is blooming; like a spring daffodil,

And I pray it continues to keep warming the hearts of many.

PAUSE

I am a nocturnal creature, and my best poetry is created....

When I am not exposed to sunlight.

PAUSE

This is why I am continually writing under the night sky.

Maybe that's why I am destined to shine.

Just like the second brightest star.... Canopus.

AM I AN ARTIST?

Am I like Picasso because I put my art on a canvas? Am I like Mozart because I create poetic symphonies, or am I just like Dynamo because I turn my words into magic?

Rico Coombs

POETIC ROYALTY

Poetic royalty

Poetic elite

Poetry minus a beat

Is that the word on the street

Rhyming couplets and similes

Onomato-

PAUSE

Poeia

Alliteration

Excuse the above abbreviation

Exclamation mark

Metaphorically

I'm using figurative speech

One may say figurative language

Ironically

The irony

Is ironic

You can call the above a sandwich

Minus the lettuce or mayo

Maya Angelou

Rest in Peace.

I'm saddened the deceased can't see what I achieved

But I believe one day we will meet

At Jesus' feet.

TALENT INSPIRES GREATNESS

Talent Inspires Greatness; which is the reason why I surround myself around official personnel.

I inked my motto on my arm… to always keep me continually motivated towards my dreams.

I tell people to live the life that they love, which is why when the city is sleeping, I'm up burning the midnight lamp, writing down my aims and drawing my objectives.

One day my hard work will pay off;

Just the same way my student loan will be "expunged".

I've trained myself to be disciplined like a solider marching on the beat.

That's why tunnel vision is essential, and distractions and sidetracks must be eradicated just like my "frenemies".

My heart is in my art form; like how Wendy's heart is in mines.

Whether it's private performances, public shows or creating poems for others,

My enthusiasm for my art form will never die down.

The impact of my words,

My sentences and rhymes have on the population

Motivates me to keep inspiring my generation and also both the younger and older folks.

Whether it's changing an individual's outlook on life or encouraging them to write,

I'm honoured and also humbled that an ordinary wordsmith can have such an impact from a selection of words.

I can't stop;

I won't stop;

And will never stop my talent, because it has inspired me to greatness too.

Rico Coombs

FIRE IN THE BOOTH

I feel like this is a fire in the booth

No plaster

Rhythm, rhyming and similes

Oozing from my veins, arteries and capillaries

With my pen in my hands it's military

I murder the pen like I'm on a killing spree

I'm from the home of grime

Where Dizzee, Ghetts and Kano

Are worshipped literally

For their flow, word content & delivery

I hope I can mirror even half of their success in the sector of English literacy

Poetry is my mission-ary

To expand students' vocabulary

Woe is me

I'm cold

Metaphorically

Writing poetry is my odyssey

I've got a confession

I love poetry unconditionally

Rico Coombs

FOR THE SAKE OF IT

I write for the sake of it

I write to escape for a bit

I write regularly, some may call it a habit

I fly annually, because I'm used to it

HONEY FROM THE HONEYCOMB

The sweetness of honey; fresh from the honeycomb.

It could rot your teeth with the content of the natural sugars.

Pure and golden, when the light reflects on it, glistening.

Tireless worker bees… work to make the organic spring blossom honey, for humans to enjoy and indulge.

Yet humans don't understand, and can't comprehend the energy and effort which the bees put into it; to deliver what we enjoy and indulge in.

A master class of teamwork; a master class of craftsmanship.

To deliver what is used for our sweet dishes and cereals.

Honey sweet from the honeycomb.

Rico Coombs

MUSIC IS HIS PASSION

Music is his passion

Music is his life

Music is his companion

And music is his wife

From singing high notes to vocal keys

Neighbours know his name

But he ain't Tremaine Neverson

Google that

PAUSE

October's very own but he wasn't born in May

18th August is his birth-day

This ain't no wordplay

NEVER KNEW I WOULD GET THIS FAR

Truthfully, I never believed that my poetry would take me to this current destination.

I never once doubted myself or my ability...

It's humbling.

Yet still too amazing to see how my words have touched the hearts of many.

People keep telling me my poetry has touched the hearts of countless individuals.

To be honest, I never knew my parker pen would take me this far.

I'm starting to get global attention for my work via word of mouth and the use of social media.

I guess those sleepless nights writing poetry under the candlelight is starting to pay off.

When I was a juvenile, if I was told that...

My work would be read by many,

I would have never believed it.

But I guess I believed in my own ability, so I shall succeed.

I should have been ready for what the future has in store for me.

They said hard work and determination pays off, I guess I'm living proof.

Now I'm diversifying my talent and putting my vocals to music, while spitting in the booth.

I'm continuing to make my pen pierce my notepad, and watch the ink dry on the white piece of paper.

My passion lies in the arts of making words into a poetic melody.

Without poetry I would feel...

Useless, like an Eagle

Without his WINGS.

OCTOBER'S VERY OWN

October's very own

But I'm a May born

Success driven

That's the cornerstone

Months of hard work

About to be paid off

Excitement and adrenaline running high

Anticipating the grand finale is nearby

Sleepless nights have been the sacrifice for our success

No one believed

Yet we have achieved

Against the odds

Dimmed lighting but our ambition is radiant

Different agendas but the same goal

Trial and error has been our learning curve

It's been a learning experience

And an experience gained

We do it not for the money nor for the fame

But just so people can associate our passions with our last names

The objective is to uplift and inspire

Spark the flame

Ignite the fire

To make everyone around us… dream their reality

To inspire success and make it their normality

POETICALLY EPIC

Anything that I write is EPIC

Some may call it POETIC

Rico you're SICK

Call me DIABETIC

That's why I am in need of a MEDIC

It's going to be an EPIDEMIC

They call me Hyper Coombs because my POETRY

Is upbeat and ENERGETIC

Rico Coombs

FOOD FOR THOUGHT

It's a small world but a big universe.

Life is very interesting;

I'm starting to analyse it bit by bit.

In this world, we all are born alone, and we all will die alone too.

Certain situations have taught me that friends and family who we have come to love and trust are not who we thought they were.

Is life what you make it, or are our lives dictated before we are formed in the uterus?

RIVALRY

When friends become rivals,

Using underhanded tactics prevails;

Moral and ethics are a thing of the past.

Months of friendship crumbled to rubble;

I'll let time play its course.

I'm the play maker, I'm now the Hazard for the opposition's team's defence.

They say silence is golden,

Which is why my lips are sealed and I'm observant

Until I'm ready to pounce on my prey.

Like how a tiger leaps as the precise moment to strike the final blow

To eradicate its prey.

GREENER ON THE OTHER SIDE

The grass isn't greener on the other side

But that's your perception

Now that's where you want to reside

You had warmth…shelter…and protection

Out in the wilderness

Out in the cold

I had your back, but you just couldn't see it

Too old for this drama

Too old for this role play

Not to sound big headed but….

I was your saviour

I was your rescuer

When you were a damsel in distress

I formed a team around you to help get you out of this mess

But you let your emotions get the better of you

We were once part of a team

But you axed yourself from the squad

You sealed your destiny

You sealed your fate

I hope life treats you well

I hope life treats you good

I hope you learn from lives lessons

PAUSE

I wish I would.

BREAKING POINT

Breaking point; I'm at breaking point.

Pacing up and down; this thought in my head, but I can't let it go.

Dead or alive; what will be my ultimate decision.

You never knew these thoughts where in my cranium; on the exterior,

I smile while my mind is working overtime.

Breaking point; I'm at breaking point.

Liquor in my hand; I'm drinking to numb the pain.

I'm drowning my sorrows with every sip of my cup.

M.O.B but this one took my heart; yet still I told myself it would never occur.

I'm shattered like a glass; I feel empty like a window without a frame.

This pain is unbearable; but I'm soldiering it through because I brought myself up to be militant.

Thinking about domestics and a catalogue of the deceased triggers me over the edge.

FACING TIME

A prisoner to my thoughts…

restraining emotions.

I'm at the MERCY of her majesty,

minus a court.

Pacing up and down the corridors of my mind.

While thinking how I can walk as a free man.

Through these enormous wooden doors,

Waiting for the right time for JUSTICE to be served.

Yet paranoid of the road ahead,

thinking of a solution for my defence…

To reduce my sentence,

which is looking to be a lengthy one.

The evidence proves I'm an innocent man,

but the system is built against us,

They wanna do anything to put us in a CAN.

Deliberation between the judges.

My destiny is what they hold.

The words which they utter can seal my fate.

Waiting patiently for the verdict.

I'm asking for divine intervention:

"Lord God it better be a positive one".

With hands clenched together,

my eyes looking heaven bound.

But my eyes are only greeted to the enormous white ceiling,

this court may be my last chance of freedom.

Currently incarcerated.

I need to think of a method.

I need to think of a means to escape.

REASON

Everything happens for a reason.
Hardship and hard times happen for a season.
They motivate you to push harder to our achievements.
Giving up
Giving in is an act of terror,
It's an act of treason.
Because success is our motto,
Our pledge,
To success we swear our allegiance.

STRESS

People say life is full of too much stress and strain.

I guess they never took the time to analyse the saying;

NO PAIN..... NO GAIN

Stress is an issue which we all have to deal with.

We just have to make sure it doesn't control us and dictate our lifestyle.

If so, then failure is paramount.

Stress is there to test us to see if we really deserve to achieve our desired objective.

When you look back at the accomplishments you have achieved in life;

You appreciate them more based on the time, energy, effort and even in some cases, the money you put in to make your dream a reality.

Think about an objective you achieved under stress.

Now....

Imagine if you didn't achieve that objective under no stress.

Would you appreciate the outcome the same way, how you currently do, TODAY.

The stress and strains in your life make you who you are TODAY.

So, from this day forth, don't look at stress as something negative but something which empowers you, and makes you stronger.

MIRROR, MIRROR ON THE WALL...

Mirror, Mirror on the wall...

What kind of man do you see?

PAUSE

I see a man, who doesn't give up in the face of adversity.

You don't throw the towel in at life's obstacles and boulders, which you were presented with.

Regardless of the stress and strain you were going through after your mother's death,

You used your experience and your loss to motivate you; to achieve and surpass people's expectations

....of what you could accomplish.

I admire you for walking around with a smile on your face when you were in agony and pain;

And YET STILL having tunnel vision to obtaining success.

You are a man who doesn't let life's downs de-motivate him; instead, you always look at the positives, even in a negative situation.

Rico, you are a man who believes in his own dreams and visions; and you have now published your second book for all to read.

I admire your character and charisma and your smile, which lights up a room.

I also like the fact that you think your jokes are funny and even when, evidently, they are not.

CLOSURE

Closure, Closure; I never want you to leave me; but I've come to terms that you're gone.

I never processed my hurt and emotions up to this very day.

I haven't mourned at your passing, and recently I have entered into a mini-depression that I mask from the world as I don't want them to see.

On my drunken nights in the city of my birth; I always wish you were here

When I have too much liquor to drink.

I know I gotta let you go, and we both know it's to help me grow.

But I know you're guiding me; and watching over me and the steps and decisions that I make in life.

Although I am travelling life's road alone, your presence will forever be there.

Day after day, it has become easier; but sometimes I randomly ponder and imagine how life would be if you were here.

Death has taken away my life; but I am determined it will not take: my strength, drive, and fight.

I am working to get closure and hopefully one day soon I will achieve my destiny.

R.I.P

WONDERING

I wonder if I have made her PROUD, in her ABSENCE.

Even though you're light years away,

Your presence is ever close,

I know you're looking over the ones who share your DNA;

Even though you haven't been formally introduced.

CHILD OF DESTINY

I'm a money maker; you could call that ludicrous.

I've been this way ever since I came out of my mother's uterus.

That why I am turning my five p's into fivers,

I am on the road to success minus a driver.

My dream is to be pushing a Range, but I am currently pushing a Mirca.

My lifetime aims and objectives are synchronized... minus a pool and a diver.

I'm a child of destiny;

So does that make me a survivor?

OYSTER

They say the world is your oyster,

Yet Londoners

Have it in their back pocket.

But people don't utilise it for its full potential.

It unlocks barriers,

Gives you the opportunity

To arrive and explore amazing destinations.

It is the gateway to London's Heathrow, Gatwick, City, Luton, and Stanstead airports.

It is our passport to different cultures, customs and currencies and continental cuisines.

Unfortunately, only a fragment of the population

Has arrived or departed from those international gateways of exposure.

Rico Coombs

FREEDOM OF SPEECH

I'm not one to take my shoes and socks off on a British beach.

But it's for inspiration, which is why I have titled this poem: freedom of speech.

So, here goes nothing...

I speak to the waves but hear no verbal response.

Yet still I hear water at full focus crashing against the gigantic rocks.

What is the definition of the term freedom of speech?

Does it mean speaking what is on my mind, at any location, regardless of the date or time?

If so, that means I'm within the guidelines and I'm still eligible to write this rhyme.

I walk on the beach at night and speak my mind.

No one can tell me to shut up...

To be quiet...

Or lower my tone.

It's freedom of speech and I am in my poetic zone.

I'm one with nature, I'm one with the sea.

I'm speaking out loud and the waters understand me.

It hears me speak and listens to my every word attentively.

It feels my pain but still doesn't respond to my agony.

It's freedom of speech, so no verbal response is needed.

Yet still the pebbles are my audience...

And the sea is my crowd.

It's freedom of speech, so it doesn't question me if I speak out loud.

Rico Coombs

GOOD OLD DAYS

What happened to da good old days?

Where children got on the bus for 40p?

And when da older generation used to use the phrase, "you're barking up the wrong tree."

Where clubs were fight-free and Brits used to drink Tetley tea.

Where young people's future was bright; like Sean Paul's smash single, Gimme da light.

What happened to da good old days when people just used to debate?

Now people have to choose their words carefully, or it could seal their fate.

Back in da good old days, everyone you knew was your sister and brother.

Now everyone is moving suspicious and undercover.

Back in da good old days, people's faces never resembled Leonardo Da Vinci's artistic piece da Mona.

But have you taken time to observe Londoner's persona?

In da good old days, there was a peaceful atmosphere.

Where people lived in peace and harmony, not in violence or fear?

Stuff has changed and has become deranged, is there ever going to be a change?

Bring back da good old days, that's a fact.

Where boys had each other's back.

Rico Coombs

THE MOTHERLAND

We pray for better days.
But we know the result.
We pray for freedom from MENTAL SLAVERY.
But in the motherland, the physical form is rapidly increasing.
We sign petitions online and post pictures on our social media pages.
But are we being part of the solution, or just bringing increased awareness to the problem?
Is prayer the solution?
Is it really going to change the situation at hand?

PLAY FAIR

I'm from a city where people don't play fair.
While the rich live up in Mayfair,
The poor play the lotto and hope to become a million-aire.
I'm from a city where everything is laid bare.
And when you used to walk through Shakespeare,
You'd have to mumble the Lord's Prayer.
Mum used to tell me to take care,
Because outside was a mine field.
Solitaire.
I'm from a city were
Pak's is the choice for most women's hair care.
Where fiends are on the corner
Asking people for welfare.
When I tell certain people about life for some…they look at me in despair…
As they were unaware of the situation here.
That some people in London actually live a NIGHTMARE.

Rico Coombs

LESSON OF LIFE

If you play with fire, you will get burnt

If you don't hear, you will feel… then you will learn.

If Naiylah doesn't hear…

She will feel, she will have to learn.

I give her unconditional love, but I still have to be stern.

If you make a mistake in life, take the next U-turn.

Knowledge is power.

That's why my mother paid for my education each term.

That's why there is an increase in university tuition every term.

Politicians lie that the public is their concern.

If their lies were brought forth to a court of law, it would be adjourned.

But if a man commits a crime to better himself or his family,

He will get the full term.

ATLANTIC

In the midst of the Atlantic Ocean,

Above the heavens,

Yet below eternity,

Are the exact coordinates of our location,

3050 miles away from London.

Courtesy of a man-made majestic metallic bird.

I sleep as a babe upon a mother's breast.

I arose abruptly from my angelic slumber,

Staring death in the face,

Yet having barely experienced life.

The force,

The impact,

Of being toyed by the elements,

Had my heart pondering

Constantly and vigorously swayed from side

To side.

I gasp,

My heart rapidly increased,

Yet the plane,

The passengers around me sleeping… heavenly.

I felt as though destiny was about to seal my fate and my fellow passengers.

In that time frame, I told my loved ones…. I love them unconditionally.

I offered a few words into eternity…. which was a prayer.

My communication to my maker,

Asking forgiveness based on my immoral ways.

Asking God to bring us home safely, and not to abandon us at Sea.

Was my final request,

My only plea.

AM I AN ARTIST BY BIRTH

Am I an artist by birth, or nature?

By practice or behaviour?

Do I have a talent which I have been blessed with?

Or a skill which I have developed

Am I gifted,

Or is my artistry something which I have attained?

Is my poetry my craft

Or my passion?

I am regularly asked this question,

But no words ever exit my lips.

I respond with silence.

JAMAICAN VIBE

I've got the Jamaican vibe in my heart and my bloodstream.

I'm going to be legendary like the Jamaica national bobsled team.

I want to have a positive impact like Marcus Messiah Garvey and reggae's veteran Bob Marley.

Jamaica is a small island with a great impact… and loved by millions, that's a fact.

Jamaica is the Caribbean's top destination and tourist's top reservation.

With pride and joy, I wave the national flag like Bolt and Powell.

To me the gold, green and black are a part of me like how consonant is to vowel.

Jamaica leaves me speechless at her beauty; the best way to describe her is she is a rare and unique cutie.

Jamaica is so nice, and I don't know what more I can say about this sun kissed paradise.

My love for Jamaica is so surreal; I'm attracted to her tropical appeal.

Jamaica is my home until I die, even though I talk with a "Cockney "accent on a sly.

OUTRO

A journey is defined as "an act of travelling from one place to another".

Creating Voice of Expression has been a journey of pressure, self-critique, and growth, which has enabled MY poetic elevation. It has also been a challenging and prolonged journey in achieving my vision—that Voice of Expression to be a masterpiece greater than its predecessor. Frustration has been a key emotion in this journey, as I have procrastinated and doubted myself, which have played major parts in the delay of publishing this book. With understanding that the creative process takes time, many years have passed since I have been able to greet my patient and supportive audience.

I have missed the energy and buzz I receive from the impact of my poetry, and I want to savour this moment for a lifetime.

This journey has not been one which I have travelled alone on; various loved ones have taken the time to offer me suggestions, critique my work, offer and signpost me to opportunities and have even read my work through email and WhatsApp. Some of you have even been serenaded with fresh poetic pieces which I have written at the crack of dawn. Words cannot express my gratitude for you being in my life and part of my journey. Muchas gracias queridos, which translates from Spanish to English, means "thank you loved ones." I wanted to give you all a special thanks, and I believe saying in Spanish has much of a personal connection between me and you all, as I love the Spanish language.

To my well-wishers, associates, and the public at large, you challenge me to be a better poet and a writer, as I have to impress and continue to re-invent myself for you all. I feel as though I have to surprise you and gain your admiration, which enables me to continue to grow and push myself. For this I say thank you.

My outro would not be complete without thanking the person who has blessed me with this talent. A lot of people call him various names, but I'll stick with the basic one of God, and I give him admiration and praise for giving me this talent.

To the magnificent individual who gave birth to me and raised me for nineteen years, you have been part of my journey from my first exposure to poetry, until this present hour. Words don't express my love, thanks, and gratitude for always encouraging me to write, share, and showcase my work. Mummy, you have given me the confidence to make "Voice of Expression" my reality.

Te quiero, Mama x

Printed in the United States
by Baker & Taylor Publisher Services